THE BEST 50

BROWN BAG LUNCHES

Beth and Rick Renaud

BRISTOL PUBLISHING ENTERPRISES
San Leandro, California

ISBN 1-55867-234-6
Design layout: High Technology Solutions, S. A. de C. V.
Cover design: Frank J. Paredes
Cover photography: John A. Benson
Illustration: Shanti L. Nelson
Food styling: Susan Devaty
Project editor: Lisa M. Tooker

ABOUT BROWN BAG LUNCHES

Brown bag lunches aren't just for kids. No matter how old you are, bringing your lunch to work or school is an inexpensive, healthy and practical alternative to eating out. But don't let portable meals keep you chained to your desk. Lunch in a bag gives you the freedom to dine wherever you choose. Take your little brown bag and travel to the park, courtyard, river or anywhere you enjoy. Find some pleasant nooks and crannies around your workplace or school, where you can get away from ringing phones and computer screens—and delight in your homemade creations.

Variety is the key to portable lunches. If you're in a slump because you're tired of eating the same peanut butter and jelly sandwiches—or if you're at a loss for quick, creative ideas, then this is the book for you! You will find 50 fast and tantalizing reasons to look forward to lunchtime.

ANATOMY OF THE BROWN BAG LUNCH

Let's peek into our brown bag and find out how to prepare a balanced and tasty meal. You'll find each recipe includes a main course, like a sandwich, salad or leftover; a crunch of chips or crackers; and a fruit or veggie. Sometimes there's even a bonus sweet treat for those who have a sweet tooth or need a lunchtime pick-me-up.

We suggest some of our favorite crunches and fruits to accompany each main course, but you can select some of your own favorites too; or try our combos out for starters and then get crazy. You can also switch and swap recipe items and, before you know it, you'll have your very own top 100 brown bag lunches to choose from.

Each recipe makes enough for one lunch, but increase your ingredients and you can prepare lunches for the whole family!

TOOLS OF THE TRADE

Not every lunch requires utensils, a plate or bowl, but if you've packed a soup or salad, you'll want to have some things handy. We suggest keeping a whole set of tools at work so you're always prepared for the day's lunch specials.

It's always a good idea to keep a few extra napkins, salt and pepper, or maybe a little homemade allspice, handy in one of your desk drawers.

THE BASICS

Keep a set of utensils, a plate, a bowl, and even a plastic cup and coffee mug in your workspace. Try bringing some colorful pottery to work to add some style and pizzazz to your lunch hour. Just remember that with a few preparations and the proper gear, you can travel with your favorite meals anywhere.

CARRYING CASES

While the brown bag is classic, lunch boxes reduce waste and prevent the "squash" factor—all while making a statement. It's never too late for that super-hero lunch box you always wanted as a kid.

For many food items, sealed plastic containers serve as the best choice for a practical, spill-proof and crisp-retaining way to travel with salads, dressings, leftovers and liquid side items. And then there are the new nylon, brown-bag-shaped lunch totes that are reusable, colorful, fairly insulating, and tough enough to keep your lunch upright.

THE ACCOMPANIMENT

Each selection in *The Best 50* revolves around a main course. With each of these, we include suggestions for a crunch, fruit and/or veggie, and sometimes a sweet snack. But we encourage experimentation. The following is a basic list of sides for mixing and matching to your taste. Enjoy!

CRUNCH:

potato chips, pretzels
popcorn
potato sticks
graham crackers
breadsticks
crackers, crackers and cheese
rice cakes

cookies
peanuts
granola bars
chips and salsa
tortilla chips
saltines

FRUIT AND VEGGIES:

apple
sliced apple and cinnamon
orange
pear
peach
plum
banana
grapes
fruit salad
berries
melon
grapefruit
nectarine
Mandarin orange
tangerine

kiwi
mango
pineapple
raisins
dried apricots
cottage cheese and pineapple
fruit yogurt
celery and peanut butter
celery and cream cheese
celery and cheese
carrots
cucumbers in vinegar
pickles
fruit bars
fruit slices

ROAST BEEF SALAD SANDWICH

If you enjoy tuna and chicken salad sandwiches, then it's time to try this roast beef salad for a new delicious "sandie!"

1-2 tbs. mayonnaise
1 tbs. pickle or celery relish
2-4 slices roast beef
2 slices sourdough bread
1 leaf lettuce

Combine mayonnaise and relish with ground roast beef in a blender or process with a food processor. Blend until smooth. Spread on bread and place lettuce on top. Makes 1 serving.

Crunch: potato chips

Fruit: red apple

ROAST BEEF AND HAVARTI DILL

When you put these mouth-watering ingredients into a sandwich, you may want to consider making a few extras to share with co-workers, or you could find them gone! This sandwich combo is a longtime favorite in the wine country.

1 tbs. Dijon mustard
1 crisp roll
2-3 slices roast beef
2-3 slices Havarti with dill
1 leaf lettuce
$1/2$ cup alfalfa sprouts

Spread Dijon evenly on roll halves. Top with roast beef, Havarti, lettuce and sprouts. Makes 1 serving.

Crunch: pretzels

Veggie: celery

ROAST BEEF RUSSIAN STYLE

For a great variation, try adding some cole slaw to this creation.

1 tbs. Russian dressing
2 slices light rye bread
2-3 slices roast beef
2-3 slices cheddar cheese
2 slices tomato
1 leaf lettuce

Spread dressing evenly on each slice of bread. Top with roast beef, cheese, tomato and lettuce. Makes 1 serving.

Crunch: sesame breadsticks

Veggie: carrots

AVOCADO, BACON, LETTUCE AND TOMATO

This sandwich is as easy-to-prepare as 1-2-3.

1-2 tbs. Thousand Island dressing
2 slices dark rye bread
3 slices bacon, cooked
2-4 slices avocado
2 slices tomato
2 leaves crisp lettuce

Spread dressing evenly on rye halves. Top with bacon, avocado, tomato and lettuce. Makes 1 serving.

Crunch: salted tortilla chips and salsa

Fruit: pear

Sweet: butter cookies

BACON-IT-EASY

Put a few extra pieces of bacon in the pan on Sunday morning, and enjoy your foresight by creating something extra for Monday afternoon.

1-2 tsp. butter
2 slices white bread
2-3 tbs. crunchy peanut butter
2-3 slices cooked bacon, crumbled

Lightly butter bread and spread peanut butter evenly on each slice. Top with bacon. Makes 1 serving.

Crunch: saltines

Fruit: red apple

SWEET-AND-SOUR CHICKEN SALAD SANDWICH

Take chicken salad in a new, delicious direction.

1-2 tbs. Tiger Sauce or any bottled
spicy sweet-and-sour sauce
1 chicken breast
2 slices oat bread
1/8 cup chopped green bell pepper
1/8 cup chopped red onion
1-2 tbs. mayonnaise
1 leaf lettuce
salt and pepper to taste

Heat sweet-and-sour sauce over medium heat. Add chicken to skillet and sauté until done. Set aside chicken to cool. Chop chicken and combine with peppers, onion and mayonnaise. Spread evenly on each slice of bread. Top with lettuce. Sprinkle lightly with salt and pepper. Makes 1 serving.

Crunch: honey nut mini-rice cakes
Fruit: pear

SANDWICHES WITH MEAT

THE DAY-AFTER DELIGHT

You'll give thanks when you try this classic post-Thanks-giving Day recipe.

1 tbs. mayonnaise
1 crisp roll or 2 slices Syrian bread
2-3 slices roasted turkey
salt and pepper to taste
$\frac{1}{2}$ cup stuffing
1-2 tbs. cranberry sauce

Spread mayonnaise on roll or bread slices. Layer with turkey and sprinkle with salt and pepper. Top second layer with stuffing and cranberry sauce. Makes 1 serving.

Crunch: potato chips

Sweet: apple pie

CHICKEN SALAD WITH PINEAPPLE

If you're looking for a tropical delight, try this island favorite.

1 tbs. olive oil
1 cup chopped cooked chicken
1/3 cup crushed pineapple, well drained
1/3 cup mayonnaise
1/8 cup chopped walnuts
1 crisp roll
1 leaf iceberg lettuce
salt and pepper to taste

Heat oil in a skillet over medium heat. Add chicken and sauté until done; or bake at 375° for 30 minutes. Set aside to cool. Combine chicken, pineapple, mayonnaise and walnuts. Spread evenly on roll halves. Top with lettuce. Add salt and pepper to taste. Makes 1 serving.

Variation

For a tangy addition, try replacing the mayonnaise with $1/4$ cup of sour cream and 1 tablespoon of cider vinegar.

Crunch: mini-pretzels

Fruit: Granny Smith apple

CHICKEN SALAD WITH RED GRAPES

If dry chicken sandwiches have thrown you off the chicken-sandwich-wagon, then try this one.

1 tbs. olive oil
1 cup chopped chicken
1/3 cup red grapes, halved
1/8 cup chopped onion
1 tbs. mayonnaise
2 slices wheat bread
1 leaf lettuce
salt and pepper to taste

Heat oil in a skillet over medium heat. Add chicken and sauté until done; or bake at 375° for 30 minutes. Set aside to cool.

Combine chicken, grapes, onion and mayonnaise. Spread evenly on each slice of bread. Top with lettuce and add salt and pepper to taste. Makes 1 serving.

Crunch: wheat crackers and cheddar cheese

Fruit: red apple

TURKEY GOLD CLUB

Turn the regular "club" up a notch with this fruity surprise. Membership does have its privileges.

2 tsp. mayonnaise
2 slices white bread
2-3 slices turkey

2-3 slices bacon, cooked
2-3 slices golden pear
2 slices tomato
1 leaf lettuce

Spread mayonnaise evenly on each slice of bread. Top with remaining ingredients. Makes 1 serving.

Crunch: graham crackers

Fruit: red grapes

ANTIPASTO IN A SANDWICH

As good as this one is plain, it's even better toasted.

1 tbs. olive oil
2 slices crusty Italian bread
4 slices prosciutto
$1/4$ cup chopped roasted red and yellow bell peppers
2 slices provolone cheese
chopped fresh basil for sprinkling

Lightly brush bread with olive oil, and grill in toaster oven. Top with remaining ingredients. Makes 1 serving.

Sides: Gourmet green olives; premade salad in a sealed plastic container with Italian dressing on the side

Fruit: red grapes

CHICKEN CAESAR SALAD SANDWICH

Beware of the hungry co-worker when you bring this one to the office. This sandwich is popular with fans of Caesar salad.

1 tbs. olive oil
1 cup chopped chicken
1-2 tbs. Caesar dressing
1 bulky roll
2 tbs. shredded Parmesan cheese
1 leaf romaine lettuce

Heat oil in a skillet over medium heat. Add chicken and sauté until done, or bake at 375° for 30 minutes. Set aside to cool. Combine chicken and dressing. Spread mixture on bread, sprinkle with Parmesan cheese and top with lettuce. Makes 1 serving.

Crunch: breadsticks

Fruit: green grapes

SUMMER HAM AND SWISS

Don't let the name fool you—this lunch will rock your world any time of the year.

$^1/_2$ tbs. mustard
$^1/_2$ tbs. mayonnaise
2 slices light rye bread
2-3 slices baked ham
2 slices Swiss cheese
4 slices cucumber

Combine mustard and mayonnaise. Spread mixture evenly on each slice of bread. Top with remaining ingredients. Makes 1 serving.

Crunch: saltines

Fruit: apple slices and cinnamon

NEW ENGLAND HAM AND CHEESE

If you've ever sat on a sunny New England hillside on a crisp autumn day, one bite of this sandwich will take you back there.

1 tbs. honey mustard
1 bulky roll
2-3 slices baked ham
2 slices cheddar cheese
2-3 slices apple

Spread honey mustard evenly on roll halves. Top with remaining ingredients. Makes 1 serving.

Side: pineapple cottage cheese with wheat crackers

THE LITTLE BO PEEP

Try this one out the day after a holiday feast, and you'll be glad that Bo Peep never found her sheep.

1/4 cup butter, softened
1 tsp. curry powder
2 slices marble rye bread
2-3 slices roast lamb

Combine butter and curry. Spread mixture evenly on each slice of bread. Top with lamb. Makes 1 serving.

Crunch: potato chips

Fruit: red apple slices

HARBORMASTER SANDWICH

Try this sandwich and you won't believe the taste. You can create more variations by using different cheeses or sauces.

3 cold meatballs, halved
2 slices whole wheat or rye bread
1-2 tbs. gravy
2-3 slices Havarti cheese
2 slices tomato
1 leaf lettuce
1 pinch parsley

Place meatballs on each slice of bread and spread gravy evenly over meatballs. Top with remaining ingredients. Makes 1 serving.

Crunch: potato chips

Veggie: carrots and celery

SWISS TUNA

If you're the type who gets spoiled easily, you may not want to risk trying this. A plain tuna sandwich will never be the same again!

½-1 cup water-packed tuna, drained
1-2 tbs. mayonnaise
2 slices light rye bread

2-3 slices cooked bacon
2 slices Swiss cheese
2 slices tomato

Combine tuna and mayonnaise. Spread mixture evenly on each slice of bread. Top with bacon, cheese and tomato. Makes 1 serving.

Crunch: tortilla chips and salsa

Fruit: red apple

DAD'S DILL TUNA

You're in for a thrill with this legendary version of a tuna "sandie."

1/2-1 cup water-packed tuna, drained
1-2 tbs. mayonnaise
1/8 cup chopped celery
1/8 cup chopped onion
1 tbs. pickle juice
2 slices white bread

Combine tuna, mayonnaise, celery, onion and pickle juice. Spread mixture evenly on each slice of bread. Makes 1 serving.

Crunch: salt and vinegar potato chips

Veggie: pickles

BALSAMIC TUNA

A healthy tuna salad alternative, this recipe will add a real zing to your next lunch hour.

$1/2$-1 cup water-packed tuna, drained
$1 1/2$ tbs. balsamic vinegar
$1/8$ cup chopped onion
$1/8$ cup chopped green bell pepper
2 slices whole wheat bread

Combine tuna, vinegar, onion and pepper. Spread mixture evenly on each slice of bread. Makes 1 serving.

Crunch: stone wheat crackers and cheddar cheese

Veggie: carrots and celery

SPICY CORNED BEEF

An Americanized version of the Irish classic, corned beef and cabbage. You'll feel lucky to have this sandwich to look forward to at lunchtime.

1 tbs. spicy mustard
2 slices rye or pumpernickel bread
2-3 slices corned beef
$1/3$ cup cole slaw

Spread mustard evenly on each slice of bread. Top with remaining ingredients. Makes 1 serving.

Crunch: pretzels

Fruit: apple and red grapes

STACK 'EM UP

Add a few slices of avocado to this stack of veggies for an extra treat.

2-3 tbs. garlic hummus
2 slices wheat bread
4 slices cucumber
3 slices tomato
1 slice red onion
1/3 cup alfalfa or dill sprouts

Spread hummus generously on each slice of bread. Top with remaining ingredients. Makes 1 serving.

Crunch: stone wheat crackers

Fruit: green grapes

Sweet: peanut butter cookie

GARDEN HUMMUS

Hummus has its origins in the Middle East and makes a tasty addition to any sandwich.

1/4 cup garlic hummus
2 slices crusty Syrian bread
2 slices provolone cheese
4 slices cucumber
1/3 cup alfalfa or dill sprouts

Spread hummus on each slice of bread. Place cheese on hummus and top with cucumber and sprouts. Makes 1 serving.

Crunch: salt and vinegar potato chips

Fruit: navel orange

Sweet: chocolate chip cookie

JAH'VACADO DELIGHT

When you dig into this red, gold, black and green reggae-style sandwich, you'll be jammin' too.

2-3 slices avocado
2-3 slices cheddar cheese
2 slices sourdough bread
2 slices tomato
pepper to taste

Layer avocado and cheese on each slice of bread. Heat in toaster oven until cheese is slightly melted or bake at 350° for 5 to 7 minutes. Top with tomato and pepper. Makes 1 serving.

Variation

Get really wild and replace tomato with ½ cup cooked chicken.

Crunch: tortilla chips and salsa

Fruit: red apple

PESTO PANINI

Make a little extra pesto for dinner and you'll have enough leftover for this sandwich the next day.

2 tbs. pesto sauce
2 slices sourdough bread
2-3 slices cheddar cheese
2 slices tomato
1 leaf lettuce

Spread pesto sauce evenly on each slice of bread. Top with remaining ingredients. Makes 1 serving.

Crunch: saltines

Fruit: peach

PB AND PICKLE

Add a zesty pick-up to your peanut butter with this easy-to-whip-together sandwich.

2-3 tbs. crunchy peanut butter
2 slices honey oat bread
3-4 slices pickles

Spread peanut butter evenly on each slice of bread. Top with pickles. Makes 1 serving.

Crunch: potato chips

Veggie: celery

GRATEFUL GRANOLA, PEANUT BUTTER AND BANANA "SANDIE"

Reminiscent of the aluminum foil-clad sandwiches doled out at Grateful Dead concerts for a dollar, this crunchy sandwich is guaranteed to make you smile, smile, smile!

2-3 tbs. peanut butter
1 tsp. honey
2 slices oat bread
1/2 banana, sliced
1/4 cup granola

Spread peanut butter on one slice, and honey on the other. Top with banana and granola. Makes 1 serving.

Crunch: tortilla chips

Fruit: apple

HAWAIIAN SUNRISE

Enjoy a little luau at lunchtime with this tangy Polynesian pleaser.

$1/2$ cup shredded cabbage
$1/4$ cup shredded carrots
$1/4$ cup raisins
1 tbs. Miracle Whip Light Salad Dressing
2 slices whole wheat bread
2 slices or chunks pineapple
2 slices Havarti cheese
2 thick lettuce leaves

Combine cabbage, carrots, raisins and dressing. Spread mixture evenly on each slice of bread. Layer with pineapple, cheese and lettuce. Makes 1 serving.

Crunch: rice cakes

Sweet: chocolate chip cookie

PUPS IN A POCKET

This hot dog alternative is great for vegetarians or meat-lovers who want something different.

3-4 shredded sharp cheddar cheese
1 tbs. Dijon mustard
1 large soft tortilla
1½ tofu hot dogs

Sprinkle cheese and spread mustard down middle of tortilla. Cut hot dogs in half lengthwise and across in halves. Place hot dog pieces on top of cheese. Wrap burrito-style and place in a sandwich bag. Once at your destination, heat in a microwave for 45 seconds. Makes 1 serving.

Crunch: pretzels

Veggies: carrots and celery

FEEL GOOD FALAFEL

Once you decide to make this lunch, it'll keep you feeling good all day.

1 tbs. mayonnaise
1 pinch ground cumin
2 slices wheat bread
3 cooked falafel balls, halved
2 slices tomato
1 leaf lettuce

Combine mayonnaise and cumin and spread evenly on each slice of bread. Top with falafel balls, tomato and lettuce. Makes 1 serving.

Crunch: graham crackers and cream cheese

Fruit: green grapes

MEXICAN LETTUCE AND TOMATO SANDWICH

For a real fiesta, try adding beans and/or rice to this pocket. Arrrrriba!

1 tbs. salsa
1 tbs. sour cream
1 pita pocket
2-3 slices Monterey Jack cheese
2-3 slices tomato
2 leaves crisp lettuce

Combine salsa and sour cream. Cut a 1-inch section from one side of pita bread to open a pocket. Place cut sections of bread inside pocket. Stuff remaining mixture and ingredients into pocket. Makes 1 serving.

Side: yogurt

Crunch: tortilla chips

Fruit: apple

LUNCH OUT AT THE WALDORF?

This variation of the classic Waldorf salad will make you feel simply spoiled.

3-4 cups shredded iceberg lettuce
1 McIntosh or red apple, diced
¼ cup raisins
⅛ cup red cherries
⅛ cup chopped walnuts
1-2 heaping tbs. Miracle Whip Salad Dressing

Combine lettuce, apple, raisins, cherries and walnuts. Add dressing and toss. Makes 1 serving.

Note: If you're preparing a portable lunch, place salad and dressing in separate containers so the lettuce stays crisp.

Side: multi-grain bread

Crunch: saltines

Fruit: tangerine

FIELD GREEN SALAD

This salad makes a wonderful, healthy and colorful main dish for any lunchtime excursion.

3-4 cups torn mixed greens
1/8 cup dried cranberries
1/8 cup crushed walnuts
1/4 cup golden raisins
1/3 cup goat cheese
2 tbs. *Balsamic Vinaigrette Dressing*

BALSAMIC VINAIGRETTE DRESSING
1 clove garlic, chopped
1 1/2 tsp. honey
1 1/2 tsp. balsamic vinegar
1/8 cup extra virgin olive oil
salt to taste

Combine all salad ingredients. Set aside. Mix dressing, pour into salad and toss. Makes 1-2 servings.

Note: If you're preparing a portable lunch, place salad and dressing in separate containers so the lettuce stays crisp.

Crunch: graham crackers

Fruit: banana

BROCCOLI SALAD

You can premix this dish, and bring to work or school in a small Tupperware container.

3 stalks broccoli
2 tbs. chopped onion
4 slices cooked bacon, crumbled
1/4 lb. fresh mushrooms, sliced
1 hard-boiled egg

DRESSING
2 tbs. vinegar
3 oz. cream cheese, softened
2 tbs. sugar
1/4 tsp. pepper
1/8 tsp. garlic salt
1 tbs. mustard
1 egg
1 tbs. vegetable oil

Cut broccoli into bite-sized pieces. Combine broccoli, onion, bacon and mushrooms. Set aside. Mix dressing ingredients, add to salad and toss. Cut egg into small pieces and sprinkle over top of salad. Makes 1-2 servings.

For variety, replace broccoli with 3-4 cups of spinach salad.

Note: Please consider using "egg substitutes" when preparing this recipe. Raw eggs have been know to cause salmonella-induced illness in some cases.

Side: roll and butter

Fruit: Mandarin orange

SPINACH SALAD

Eating this salad is not only good for you, but it is also easy to transport to your next destination.

3-4 cups fresh spinach
2 slices cooked bacon, crumbled
1/8 cup chopped onion
1/8 cup pine nuts
1/4 cup sliced mushrooms
1 hard-boiled egg, sliced
1/8 cup goat cheese, optional

DRESSING
1 tsp. red wine vinegar
1 tsp. Dijon mustard
1 tbs. olive oil
parsley to taste
thyme to taste

1 small clove garlic, chopped
salt and pepper to taste

Combine spinach, bacon, onion, pine nuts, mushrooms, egg and cheese. Set aside. Mix dressing, add to salad and toss. Makes 1-2 servings.

Note: If you're preparing a portable lunch, place salad and dressing in separate containers so the spinach stays crisp.

Crunch: breadsticks

FRUIT SALAD

When fruit is in season, there's nothing like a bowl of fresh fruit for lunch. Round out the fruit with a cup of cottage cheese or a container of plain or fruity yogurt. With salty saltines on the side—or crunchy graham crackers—you'll feel satisfied and refreshed. Top with Grape Nuts or granola, if you're feeling a bit sassy.

1-2 cups blueberries or alternate seasonal fruit
1 cup cottage cheese
1 container plain or fruit-flavored yogurt, optional
$1/2$ cup granola or Grape Nuts

Combine fruit of your choice, cottage cheese and yogurt in a bowl. Makes 1 serving.

Note: Replace blueberries with other seasonal fruits or combine with 2 or 3 favorites: strawberries, cantaloupe, kiwi, banana, watermelon, raspberries, orange, peach, nectarine, honeydew melon, blueberries, apple, grapes, banana, watermelon or kiwi.

Crunch: saltines or graham crackers

PEAR, WALNUT AND GOAT CHEESE SALAD

This salad has something for everyone with fruit and lettuce, and even a bit of cheese.

3-4 cups torn romaine lettuce
1 pear
$1/_8$ cup chopped walnuts
$1/_4$ cup shredded goat cheese

DRESSING
1 tbs. lemon juice
1 tsp. honey
1 tbs. olive oil
salt and pepper to taste

Combine lettuce, walnuts and cheese. Set aside. Mix lemon juice and salt, whisk in honey and add olive oil and pepper. Add dressing to salad and toss. Cut pear into bite-sized pieces before serving. Makes 1-2 servings.

Note: If you're preparing a portable lunch, place salad and dressing in separate containers so the lettuce stays crisp.

Crunch: dark wheat crackers

THE MEAN BEAN

This colorful salad is the perfect dish with fresh summer vegetables.

¹/₄ lb. green beans
³/₄ cup halved red cherry tomatoes
³/₄ cup sliced red and yellow bell pepper

DRESSING
1 tbs. olive oil
1 tsp. red wine vinegar
¹/₈ cup chopped onion
1 tsp. minced basil
1 tsp. minced chives
1 tbs. Dijon mustard
¹/₂ tsp. minced oregano
1-2 tsp. lemon juice
salt and pepper to taste

Steam beans in a pot over high heat until crisp-tender. Set aside to cool. Cut beans into inch-long pieces. Combine beans, tomatoes and peppers. Add salt and pepper to taste. Set aside. Mix dressing, pour into bean mixture and chill overnight.

Crunch: stone wheat crackers

GREEK SALAD

Take this salad along on your next outing. It's portable and healthy too.

3-4 cups torn iceberg lettuce
$^1/_3$ cup crumbled feta cheese
$^1/_3$ cup sliced mushrooms
2 slices onions, separated
$^1/_4$ cup black olives
2-3 tbs. Italian dressing

Combine lettuce, cheese, mushrooms, onions and olives. Add dressing and toss. Makes 1-2 servings.

Note: If you're preparing a portable lunch, place salad and dressing in separate containers so the lettuce stays crisp.

Side: pita bread

Fruit: strawberries

AVOCADO SALAD

There's nothing like a crisp salad on a warm day. Toss with dressing and enjoy!

3-4 torn red leaf lettuce
$1/2$ cup sprouts
$1/4$ cup raisins
$1/8$ cup pine nuts
$1/2$ avocado, sliced
2-3 tbs. *Balsamic Vinaigrette Dressing*, page 40

Combine lettuce, sprouts, raisins, pine nuts and avocado. Add vinaigrette and toss. Makes 1-2 servings.

Note: If you're preparing a portable lunch, place salad and dressing in separate containers so the lettuce stays crisp.

Side: peanut butter and celery

Fruit: apple

CAESAR SALAD

A Caesar salad is a favorite of many. Try this one with a few homemade croutons.

CROUTONS
1 tbs. olive oil
1 clove garlic, chopped
1 slice thick homemade bread, cubed

SALAD
3-4 cups torn romaine lettuce
$\frac{1}{3}$ cup croutons
1 tbs. anchovies, optional
$1\frac{1}{2}$ tsp. capers
$\frac{1}{8}$ cup shredded Parmesan cheese
2-3 tbs. *Caesar Dressing*, follows

CAESAR DRESSING
1 egg
1 tbs. lemon juice
1 tsp. mustard

Heat oil in a skillet over medium heat. Add garlic to skillet and sauté until soft. Add bread and brown. Drain olive oil from bread and set aside to cool. Combine lettuce, croutons, anchovies and capers. Sprinkle Parmesan on top. Whisk dressing in a small bowl, pour into salad mixture and toss. Makes 1-2 servings.

Note: If you're preparing a portable lunch, place salad and dressing in separate containers so the lettuce stays crisp. See note about use of raw eggs on page 43.

Fruit: orange

Sweet: mint cookies

TROPICAL YOGURT

Light fare with an island flavor.

1 container vanilla yogurt
$1/4$ cup drained crushed pineapple
$1/4$ cup drained Mandarin oranges
1 tbs. chopped walnuts

Combine yogurt, pineapple, oranges and walnuts. Makes 1 serving.

Crunch: cracked wheat crackers

Sweet: oatmeal cookie

YOGURT—RED, WHITE AND BLUE

This favorite is almost as American as apple pie.

1 container yogurt, any flavor
1/4 cup sliced strawberries
1/4 cup sliced nectarine
1/4 cup sliced peach
1/4 cup blueberries
1/4 cup grapes
1-2 tbs. Grape Nuts

Combine yogurt, fruit and Grape Nuts. Makes 1 serving.

Side: toasted sesame bagel with cream cheese or butter

LOXAGLE

Loxed or unloxed, it's safe to say that this "brown bagger" will surely please.

1 sesame bagel, sliced
2 tbs. cream cheese
2 pieces lox
2 rings onion
2 slices tomato

Lightly toast bagel in a toaster. Spread cream cheese evenly on bagel halves. Top with lox, onions and tomato. Makes 1 serving.

Crunch: potato chips

Fruit: apple

Sweet: chocolate chip cookie

PEPPERONI PUMPERNICKEL

Add this gourmet sandwich to your next brown bag lunch. It takes less than 2 minutes to prepare.

2 tbs. plain cream cheese
1 pumpernickel bagel, sliced
4-6 slices pepperoni

Spread cream cheese evenly on bagel halves. Place pepperoni on bagel. Makes 1 serving.

Crunch: salt and vinegar potato chips

Fruit: red pear

MINI PIZZAS

This one is strictly for those fortunate enough to have a toaster oven available at lunchtime.

2 tbs. spaghetti sauce
1 English muffin, halved
1/8 cup chopped green bell pepper, optional
1/8 cup chopped mushrooms, optional
1/8 cup chopped onion, optional
1/4 cup shredded mozzarella cheese
dried basil and pepper to taste

Spread spaghetti sauce on halved muffin. Top with peppers, mushrooms and onion. Sprinkle with cheese and add basil and pepper to taste. Cook in a toaster oven until cheese is melted and muffin is crisp, about 2 to 3 minutes. Makes 1 serving.

Side: salad with dressing on the side

MARMALADE NUT BREAD

This delicious treat goes best with a soup or salad. Premix the cream cheese and marmalade before spreading for the full effect.

2-3 tbs. softened cream cheese
2 tsp. orange marmalade
1-2 slices nut bread

Combine cream cheese and marmalade. Spread mixture evenly on nut bread. Makes 1 serving.

Side: vegetable, chicken noodle or ramen soup

Veggie: carrots

TOMATO GARLIC SOUP

If you have a plastic container or a thermos, there's no excuse for not trying this one. It's quick, healthy and very tasty.

1 can tomato soup
1-2 cloves garlic, chopped
1 tbs. hot sauce or Tiger Sauce
salt and pepper to taste

Combine soup, garlic and hot sauce. Add salt and pepper to taste. Chill for 1 hour and serve cold.

Crunch: oyster crackers

Sweet: angel food cake

LEFTOVER PASTA SALAD

Don't throw away that extra pasta! Save it for the next day and you'll have an almost ready-made lunch.

2-3 cups cooked pasta, any type
1-2 tbs. mayonnaise or light dressing
$\frac{1}{4}$ cup chopped onion
$\frac{1}{2}$ cup chopped bell peppers
$\frac{1}{4}$ cup chopped celery
salt and pepper to taste

Cut pasta into bite-sized pieces if necessary. Combine pasta, mayonnaise, onion, pepper and celery. Add salt and pepper to taste. Makes 1 serving.

Crunch: medium cheddar cheese and stone wheat crackers

Fruit: grapes

LEFTOVER POTATO SALAD

You'll never look at leftover potatoes the same way. Use last night's potatoes and you have a meal-to-go.

1 lb. potatoes
1-2 tbs. mayonnaise or any creamy dressing
1/4 cup chopped onions
1/2 cup chopped green bell peppers
1/4 cup chopped celery
1 hard-boiled egg, chopped
salt and pepper to taste

Cut potatoes into bite-sized pieces. Combine all ingredients. Makes 1-2 servings.

Crunch: breadsticks

Fruit: apple

A FUTURE FOR YOUR PASTA

Have some extra pasta leftover from last night's dinner? Try this quick, easy and delicious dish.

2-3 cups pasta, any type
1 tbs. infused oil or olive oil
1-2 tbs. grated Parmesan cheese
garlic salt and pepper to taste

Combine pasta, oil and cheese. Add garlic salt and pepper to taste. Makes 1 serving.

Side: roll and butter

Fruit: peach

_____

_____

_____

_____

_____

_____

_____

_____

_____

_____

_____
_____
_____
_____
_____
_____
_____
_____
_____
_____
_____

_____

_____

_____

_____

_____

_____

_____

_____

_____

_____

_____
_____
_____
_____
_____
_____
_____
_____
_____
_____

_____

_____

_____

_____

_____

_____

_____

_____

_____

_____

_____
_____
_____
_____
_____
_____
_____
_____
_____
_____

_____

_____

_____

_____

_____

_____

_____

_____

_____

_____

_____
_____
_____
_____
_____
_____
_____
_____
_____
_____

MY BEST BROWN BAG LUNCHES

_____

_____

_____

_____

_____

_____

_____

_____

_____

_____

_____

_____

_____

_____

_____

_____

_____

_____

_____

_____

INDEX

Antipasto in a sandwich 19
Avocado, bacon, lettuce and tomato 10
Avocado salad 53

Bacon-it-easy 11
Bacon, lettuce, tomato and avocado 10
Banana "sandie," grateful granola peanut butter 34
Bean, the mean 50
Bread, marmalade nut 61

Cheese, New England ham 22
Cheese, goat and pear, walnut 48
Chicken
  Caesar salad sandwich 20
  salad sandwich, sweet-and-sour 12
  salad with pineapple 14

salad with red grapes 16
Corned beef, spicy 28

Falafel, feel good 37
Fruit salad 46

Garlic soup, tomato 62
Grapes, red with chicken salad 16
Granola peanut butter and banana "sandie," grateful 34

Ham and cheese, New England 22
Ham and swiss, summer 21

Loxagle 58

Marmalade nut bread 61

New England ham and cheese 22
Nut bread, marmalade 61

Pasta salad, leftover 63

Peanut butter and banana "sandie," grateful granola 34
Pear, walnut and goat cheese salad 48
Pepperoni pumpernickel 59
Pesto panini 32
Pineapple, with chicken salad 14
Pizzas, mini 60

Roast beef
  and Havarti dill 8
  Russian style 9
  salad sandwich 7

Salads
  avocado 53
  broccoli 42
  Caesar 54
  field green 40
  fruit 46
  Greek 52
  leftover pasta 63

Salads, continued
  lunch out at the
    Waldorf 39
  mean bean 50
  pear, walnut and goat
    cheese 48
  spinach 44
Sandwiches
  antipasto in a 19
  avocado, bacon, lettuce
    and tomato 10
  bacon-it-easy 11
  balsamic tuna 27
  chicken Caesar salad 20
  chicken salad with
    pineapple 14
  chicken salad with red
    grapes 16
  Dad's dill tuna 26
  day-after delight 13
  feel good falafel 37
  garden hummus 30
  grateful granola peanut
    butter and banana
    "sandie" 34

harbormaster 24
Hawaiian sunrise 35
jah'vacado delight 31
Mexican lettuce and
  tomato 38
New England ham and
  cheese 22
pb and pickle 33
pesto panini 32
pups in a pocket 36
roast beef and Havarti
  dill 8
roast beef Russian style
  9
roast beef salad 7
spiced corned beef 28
stack 'em up 29
summer ham and Swiss
  21
sweet-and-sour chicken
  salad 12
Swiss tuna 25
the Little Bo Peep 23
turkey gold club 18

Soup, tomato garlic 62
Spinach salad 44
Summer ham and Swiss 21
Sweet-and-sour chicken
  salad sandwich 12

Tomato
  avocado, bacon and
    lettuce 10
  garlic soup 62
  lettuce sandwich,
    Mexican 38
Tuna
  balsamic 27
  Dad's dill 26
  Swiss 25
Turkey gold club 18

Walnut, goat cheese and
  pear salad 48

Yogurt—red, white and
  blue 57
Yogurt, tropical 56